Die Marienburg
The Marienburg

THE MARIENBURG
Life and Spirit of a House

Edited by Rolf Gerling

Translated by Jeremy Gaines

Gerling Academy Press

DIE MARIENBURG
Leben und Geist eines Hauses

Herausgegeben von Rolf Gerling

Gerling Akademie Verlag

Content

Inhalt

Alte Blutbuche im Süden des Parks   Old copper beech in the south of the park

Foreword

A manor house, a destination for day trips, a hotel complete with restaurant, the headquarters of the British occupying forces, a family seat, an office, a training center, a company guesthouse and corporate home - the Marienburg has been all of this and much more besides. It is a place of contemplation, of power, and of art. It is an impressive house, surrounded by a marvelous park. The ancient plane trees frame the Marienburg like sculptures - attesting to the forces of nature and to a place that is truly out of the ordinary.

The trees and the house are over 150 years old. For almost 70 years, the Marienburg formed the heart of life for my family. Following the death of my parents, in 1992 we converted the Marienburg into a training center and into the Gerling Group's guesthouse. In that context, the house's history proved to be a great assistance. Was the Marienburg not itself once a place of tremendous encounters? I am often asked in this connection whether I did not find it difficult to leave my family house. And I always have the same answer to offer: the Marienburg was and is a hospitable house, a place where people could relax and feel at home. Especially in view of its history, its present use is a fitting fate, a fortunate state, combining as it does representation and education, enjoyment and contemplation. The Marienburg is the Gerling Group's corporate home, a residence with a fascinating history and a future which lies in the hands of those who breath life into the house today.

If a new tree is planted in the park I try and imagine what the tree and its surroundings will look like in 50 or a 100 years' time. Whether the picture I paint before my mind's eye is then a reality is something I can never really know. And whether the picture is a fitting one is something future generations will have to decide. The same is the case with the Marienburg as a corporate home. A new idea has been seeded, a new picture arises: a lively and hospitable house, fully in the service of »the commitment to performance and success«, »the respect for man and nature«, and »the joy in beauty and creativity«.

Rolf Gerling

Vorwort

Landgut, Ausflugsort, Hotel und Restaurant, Zentrale der britischen Besatzungsmacht, Familiensitz, Büro, Bildungszentrum, Gästehaus und Corporate Home - die Marienburg war all dies und noch mehr: ein Ort der Besinnung, der Macht und der Kunst, ein eindrucksvolles Haus umgeben von einem prächtigen Park. Wie Skulpturen rahmen die uralten Platanen die Marienburg ein, zeugen von der Kraft der Natur und von einem Ort, der außergewöhnlich ist.

Bäume und Haus sind über 150 Jahre alt. Fast 70 Jahre lang war die Marienburg Lebenszentrum meiner Familie. Nach dem Tod meiner Eltern bauten wir 1992 die Marienburg zum Bildungszentrum und Gästehaus des Gerling-Konzerns um. Dabei entpuppte sich die Geschichte des Hauses als hilfreich. War die Marienburg nicht schon einmal eine erfolgreiche Stätte der Begegnung?

Ich werde in diesem Zusammenhang des öfteren gefragt, ob es mir nicht schwergefallen sei, meinen Geburtsort verlassen zu haben. Meine Antwort ist immer die gleiche: die Marienburg war und ist ein gastliches Haus, ein Ort, an dem sich Menschen wohl fühlen können. So ist ihre heutige Nutzung, auch im Hinblick auf ihre Geschichte, eine glückliche Fügung, vereinigt sie doch Repräsentation und Bildung, Freude und Besinnung. Die Marienburg ist das Corporate Home des Gerling- Konzerns, Stätte mit einer bewegten Geschichte und einer Zukunft, die in den Händen jener liegt, die das Haus heute beleben.

Wenn im Park ein neuer Baum gepflanzt wird, so stelle ich mir vor, wie sich Baum und Umfeld in den nächsten 50 oder 100 Jahren entwickeln werden. Ob sich das gewünschte Bild einstellt, ist nie vollständig vorhersehbar. Das Urteil bleibt zukünftigen Generationen überlassen. So ist es auch mit der Marienburg als Corporate Home. Eine neue Idee ist gepflanzt, ein neues Bild entsteht: ein lebendiges und gastfreundliches Haus, das im Dienste von »Wille zu Leistung und Erfolg«, »Achtung vor Mensch und Natur«, »Freude am Schönen und Gestalten« steht.

Rolf Gerling

Chapter 1
1843: The Marienburg manor house arises

Until the process of secularization which the French unleashed towards the close of the 18th century, the area which makes up the Bayenthal and Marienburg districts of Cologne belonged to the collegiate of the church of St. Severin. The lands were mainly used for agricultural purposes. Moreover, until 1782 there was also a hospital, a so-called House for the Sick, dating from the 14th century, furnished with a chapel of its own. At the end of the 18th century, merchant Johann Wilhelm Huybens had an English garden built south of the Cologne city walls - later the Alteburg Mill was erected there. And in the 1830s and 1840s, some prosperous burghers of Cologne built a small number of representative mansions before the city gates. The choice of location was most certainly influenced mainly by the attractive view of the Rhine, the wish to flee the narrow confines of the cits, and the beautiful countryside.

In October 1843, it was Paul Joseph Hagen who made the most of a favorable opportunity and acquired the lands of what was later to be the Marienburg district for the sum of 2,700 thalers by auction from the Church Elders of the Parish Church at Rodenkirchen. At the time, the lands consisted of broad fields and a ridge towards the Rhine, the Gallows Hill. The sale was made subject to the condition that within one year buildings worth at least 4,000 thalers be built there.

Paul Joseph Hagen was a merchant, a ship's chandler, and later a co-founder of the Cologne Mechanical Engineering Works in Bayenthal. He had accumulated part of his wealth by speculating on land prices and acting as a real-estate agent. After having purchased the property, Hagen had a two-story manor house built in the Classicist style. In terms of outward appearance, it resembled the summer

Kapitel 1
1843: Das Hofgut Marienburg entsteht

Bis zur Säkularisation durch die Franzosen gehörte das Gebiet, das heute die Kölner Stadtteile Bayenthal und Marienburg umfaßt, zum Herrenstift St. Severin. Es wurde hauptsächlich landwirtschaftlich genutzt. Daneben existierte noch bis 1782 ein Hospiz, ein sogenanntes Siechenhaus, aus dem 14. Jahrhundert mit Kapelle. Der Kaufmann Johann Wilhelm Huybens legte Ende des 18. Jahrhunderts südlich der Stadtmauern von Köln einen englischen Park an, in dem später die Alteburger Mühle errichtet wurde. In den 30er und 40er Jahren des 19. Jahrhunderts bauten einige wohlhabende Bürger Kölns eine kleine Anzahl repräsentativer Landhäuser vor den Toren der Stadt. Der reizvolle Blick auf den Rhein, die Flucht vor der Enge der Stadt und die schöne Landschaft waren sicherlich maßgebend für die Wahl dieses Standortes.

Im Oktober 1843 nutzte Paul Joseph Hagen eine günstige Gelegenheit, das Gelände des späteren Stadtteils Marienburg auf einer Versteigerung für 2700 Thaler vom Kirchenvorstand der Pfarrkirche zu Rodenkirchen zu erwerben. Dieses Land bestand damals aus weiten Ackerflächen und einer zum Rhein liegenden Anhöhe, dem Galgenberg. Der Erwerb erfolgte unter der Auflage, innerhalb eines Jahres Bauten im Werte von wenigstens 4000 Thalern zu errichten.

Paul Joseph Hagen war Kaufmann, Schiffsbestätter und später Mitbegründer der Kölnischen Maschinenbau Anstalt in Bayenthal. Er hatte einen Teil seines Vermögens durch Bodenspekulationen und als Makler verdient.

Nach dem Grundstückserwerb errichtete Hagen ein zweigeschossiges klassizistisches Herrenhaus. In seiner äußeren Erscheinung ähnelte es dem Sommerhaus von Friedrich Wilhelm III., das 1824/25 nach Plänen von Karl Friedrich Schinkel im Park vom

house of Friedrich Wilhelm III which was built in the park of Charlottenburg Castle to plans devised by Karl Friedrich Schinkel in 1824–5. Today, this two-story summer house is known as the »Schinkel-Pavilion«. The Marienburg was named after Anna Maria, Paul Hagen's elderst daughter.

It is not know for certain who the architect of the original Marienburg house was. Comparisons with other buildings of the time would indicate that it was the creation of Johann Peter Weyer, who was the Cologne Town Architect until 1844 and then went into private business. Alongside the »Marienburg Manor« (»Landsitz Marienburg«) - the first name of the building according to the land register - a farm, lodgings for the lessee, a bakery, a smithy, and bordering vegetable gardens and orchards were made.

The farm was leased by a farmer named Ernst Bilk. Yet the farm buildings themselves fell victim as early as 1886 to the villas that were arising in the vicinity. Today, all that alludes to the farm is the avenue »Unter den Ulmen« as the road is now called, which was the old manor entrance to the farm that was part of the Marienburg.

In 1849, speculation in real property in Cologne collapsed for the first time. Paul Joseph Hagen was one of those who lost the most and he was forced to sell the Marienburg and the associated lands to Bankhaus Sal. Oppenheim, which had the manor and farms run by a duly qualified manager.

Schloß Charlottenburg in Berlin gebaut worden war. Dieses zweistöckige Sommerhaus wird heute »Schinkel-Pavillon« genannt. Ihren Namen erhielt die Marienburg nach Anna Maria, der ältesten Tochter von Paul Hagen.

Der Architekt der ursprünglichen Marienburg ist nicht sicher bekannt. Vergleiche mit anderen Gebäuden aus dieser Zeit sprechen für Johann Peter Weyer, der bis 1844 Stadtbaumeister von Köln war und danach in die Privatwirtschaft überwechselte. Neben dem »Landsitz Marienburg« – so die erste urkundliche Bezeichnung des Hauses – entstanden ein Ackergut, eine Pächterwohnung, ein Backhaus, eine Schmiede und angrenzende Obst- und Gemüsegärten.

Die Landwirtschaft wurde von dem Landwirt Ernst Bilk gepachtet. Die hierzu gehörenden Gebäude wurden schon 1886 der Bebauung des Villenviertels geopfert. Heute erinnert nur noch eine Allee, die jetzige Straße »Unter den Ulmen«, als alte Hofzufahrt an das zur Marienburg gehörende Ackergut.

1849 kam es zu einem ersten Zusammenbruch der Kölner Grundstücksspekulationen. Paul Joseph Hagen war als einer der Hauptgeschädigten gezwungen, die Marienburg und ihre Ländereien an das Bankhaus Sal. Oppenheim zu veräußern, die das Gut durch einen Ökonomen bewirtschaften ließ.

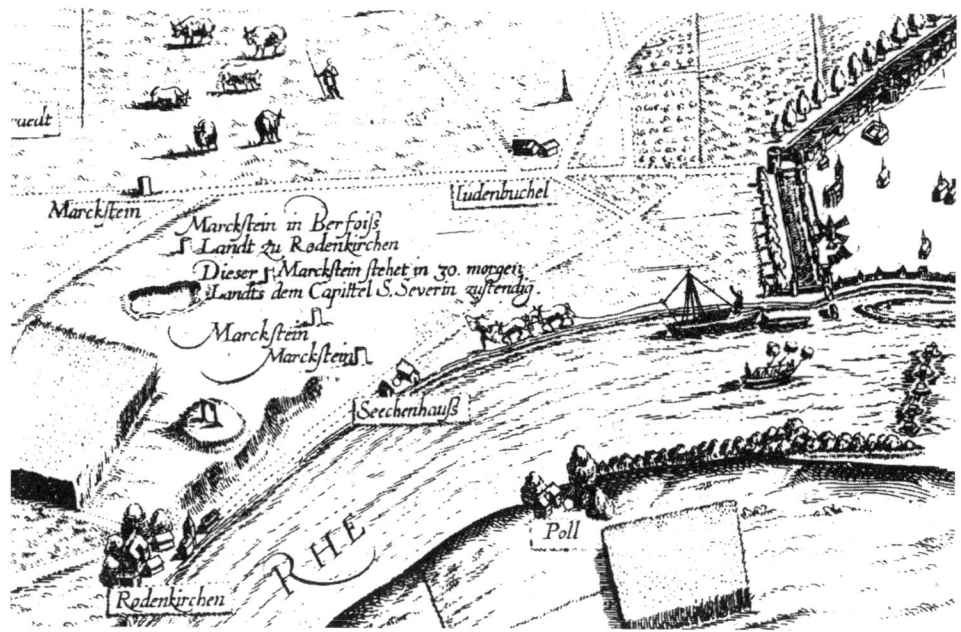

Das Gebiet des späteren Kölner Stadtteils Marienburg um 1610
The area covered by the later Marienburg district of Cologne around 1610

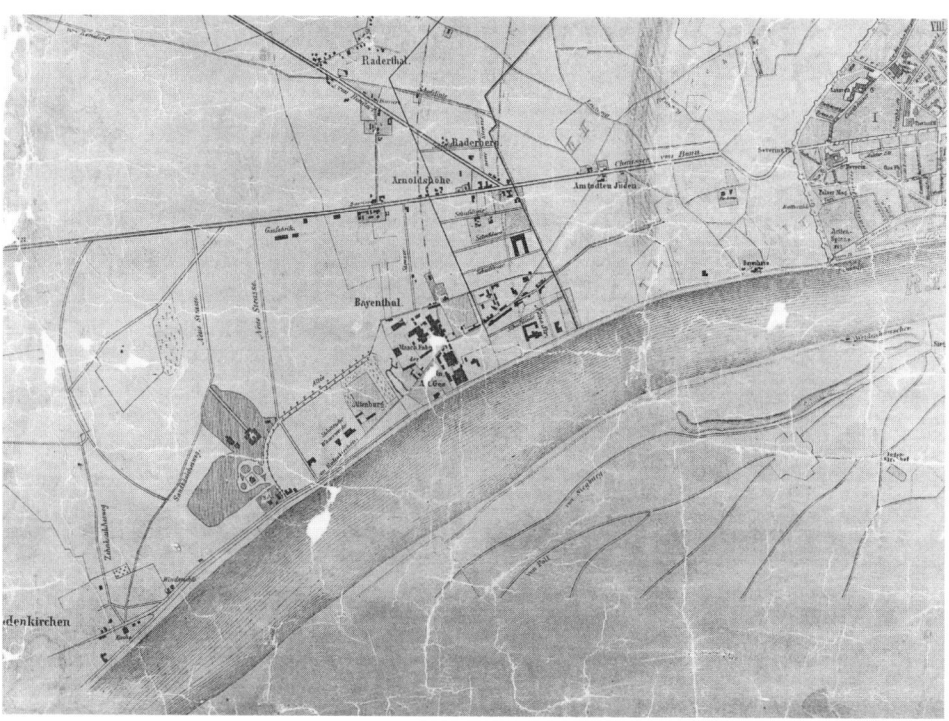

Bayenthal und Marienburg um 1877
View of Bayenthal and Marienburg around 1877

Der Schinkel-Pavillon, das Vorbild für die Marienburg

The Schinkel Pavilion, taken as the model for the Marienburg

Ostansicht der Marienburg um 1875
View of the Marienburg from the East, around 1875

Chapter 2
1867: Ernst Leybold has a vision

Minna Leybold recollects that her father discovered the Marienburg in the year 1867. »He saw, astride a hill up above the banks of the river, the Marienburg manor; it was a white, at the time unoccupied country house with green closed shutters and a flat roof in the midst of an old park, which was decidedly unkempt and had grown wild. Father's curiosity forced him onward on his voyage of discovery, and behind the manor house he came across a beautiful farm that belonged to it and broad lands which stretched as far as the Bonner Strasse and beyond. . . . My father stood there, quite alone in the vastness of the countryside and a thought shot into his head: This is the most beautiful of the spots around Cologne that has not yet been spoiled by industry. Surely here a friendly suburb of spacious villas should afford those so closely squeezed together in the city fresh air and light and country joys, without separating them from their city context.

In 1868, with support from his friend Adolph Davignon, Ernst Leybold bought the Marienburg with its outlying buildings, 50,000 square meters of parkland and some 60 hectares of fields. In 1874, Ernst Leybold and his family moved into the Marienburg Manor after it had first been carefully renovated, and it was from here that he set about making his vision of a suburb only of villas come true. Everything spoke in favor of a villa suburb being a real success. Cologne was an up-and-coming industrial center. Rapid economic growth after the foundation of the German Reich was creating much wealth there.

Until the French Revolution and the wars that followed, Cologne had been a Free Imperial City. It was then incorporated into French territory, only to be assigned to Prussia at the Vienna Con-

Kapitel 2
1867: Ernst Leybold hat eine Vision

Nach Erinnerung von Minna Leybold entdeckte ihr Vater die Marienburg im Jahre 1867: »Er sah nun am Ufer erhöht auf einem Hügel das Gut Marienburg liegen, es war ein weißes, damals unbewohntes Landhaus mit grünen geschlossenen Läden und flachem Dach inmitten eines alten Parks, der aber ungepflegt und verwildert dalag. Vater trieb die Neugierde weiter auf seiner Entdeckungsreise und er fand hinter dem Landhause eine schöne dazugehörige Oekonomie und weite Felder, die sich bis zur Bonner Straße und darüber hinaus hinziehen. ... Da stand mein Vater allein auf weiter Flur und der Gedanke schoß ihm durch den Kopf: Dies ist die schönste noch von Industrie unberührte Stelle der nahen Umgebung Kölns, hier sollte eine freundliche Villenvorstadt den in der engen Festung zusammengedrängten Menschen Luft, Licht und ländliche Freuden bringen, ohne sie von ihrem Zusammenhang mit der Stadt zu trennen.«

1868 kaufte Ernst Leybold mit Hilfe seines Freundes Adolph Davignon die Marienburg mit ihren Nebengebäuden, 50.000 qm Park und ca. 60 Hektar Felder. 1874 bezog Ernst Leybold mit seiner Familie nach gründlicher Renovierung das Gutshaus Marienburg, um von hier aus seine Vision von einer Villenkolonie zu verwirklichen. Alle Umstände sprachen für den Erfolg einer Villenvorstadt. Köln war ein aufstrebender Industriestandort. Das Wirtschaftswachstum der sogenannten Gründerjahre hatte zahlreiche neue Vermögen hervorgebracht.

Köln war bis zu den französischen Revolutionskriegen freie Reichsstadt, danach französisches Territorium und wurde durch Beschluß des Wiener Kongresses 1815 zu Preußen geschlagen. Die Stadt hatte festungsartigen Charakter. Jahrhundertelang war jeder

gress in 1815. The City resembled a fortress. For centuries, all at-
tempts to erect firm buildings in the broad fields outside the city
walls had been doomed to failure. Within the city walls, an acute
shortage of space prevailed. Since the beginning of the 19th century,
Cologne's population had almost tripled, and the populace lived sar-
dine-packed into the city area, which was itself constrained by the
city walls. In other words, there were hardly any opportunities to
live in a manner that represented one's station.

The grounds of the Marienburg had not been developed - yet
they kindled little interest among investors. This was not altered by
Leybold's unflagging efforts to press ahead with developing the villa
suburb. For example, he had a sewage network and gas pipes laid,
and tarmac roads put down. He even managed to ensure that the
Rondorf District Council's new town hall was built in 1879 in what
is now Marienburger Strasse.

The generous size of the lots was intended to ensure that only af-
fluent burghers would be interested in his »estate«. Yet developers
and buyers for the villa lots were still not forthcoming. This restraint
was probably due to the long travel times in highly uncomfortable
vehicles, not to mention the fact that the south of Cologne was almost unknown territory. »How curious that the citizens of Cologne
know and love only the Northern promenade along the Rhine as far
as the Zoological and the Flora Botanical Gardens but not one of
them is acquainted with the still undiscovered beauty up-river from
the city,« Leybold is said to have once remarked to his daughter
Minna.

Leybold's project was likewise rendered difficult by political vi-
cissitudes. Following its experiences in the 1870-1 War, the State of
Prussia ordained that the ring of fortifications around the city be extended. As part of the related measures, building permission was res-
cinded for the most beautiful section of the grounds Leybold sought
to develop, namely that along the river banks. Indeed, the buildings
that had already emerged had to be torn down again. In their place,
the Military Ring Road arose. It formed a huge semi-circle, from
the Rhine in the north to the Rhine in the south, connecting all the

Versuch vereitelt worden, feste Bauten im weiten Vorfeld der Stadtmauer zu errichten. Innerhalb der Mauern der Stadt herrschte eklatanter Flächenmangel. Seit Beginn des 19. Jahrhunderts hatte sich Kölns Einwohnerschaft fast verdreifacht und lebte dicht zusammengedrängt auf dem durch Mauern eingeschnürten Stadtgebiet. Sie bot damit kaum Gelegenheit für repräsentatives Wohnen.

Das noch unerschlossene Gelände der Marienburg stieß jedoch bei potentiellen Investoren auf wenig Interesse. Dies obwohl Leybold unermüdlich an der Entwicklung seiner Villenvorstadt arbeitete. So ließ er ein Kanalisationsnetz und Gasleitungen verlegen und befestigte Straßen errichten. Darüber hinaus konnte er durchsetzen, daß das neue Rathaus des Gemeindebezirks Rondorf 1879 in der heutigen Marienburger Straße gebaut wurde.

Eine großzügige Parzellierung der Grundstücke sollte sicherstellen, daß sich nur Wohlhabende für seine »Colonie« interessieren. Doch die Bauherren und Käufer für die Villengrundstücke ließen weiter auf sich warten. Gründe für die Zurückhaltung waren sicherlich die langen Fahrtzeiten in höchst unbequemen Verkehrsmitteln, aber auch, daß der Kölner Süden fast unbekannt war. »Wie merkwürdig, die Kölner kennen und lieben nur die nördliche Rheinpromenade zum zoologischen Garten und zur Flora, und niemand weiß, daß oberhalb der Stadt eine noch unentdeckte Schönheit liegt«, soll Leybold einmal gegenüber seiner Tochter Minna geäußert haben.

Leybolds Projekt wurde auch von politischer Seite eingeschränkt. Der preußische Staat ordnete - nach den Erfahrungen im Krieg von 1870/71 - den Ausbau des Festungsrayons rund um Köln an. Im Zuge dieser Maßnahme wurde dem schönsten – direkt am Rheinufer gelegenen - Teil des Leybold-Projekts die Bauerlaubnis entzogen und angefangene Bauten mußten wieder abgerissen werden: Die Militär-Ringstrasse wurde gebaut. Sie verband in einem großen Halbkreis vom Rhein bis zum Rhein alle Forts der Festung Köln und bildet noch heute mit ihrem südlichsten Abschnitt die Grenze des Parks der Villa Marienburg.

1880 – bereits nach fünf Jahren – gab Ernst Leybold die Marienburg als privaten Wohnsitz auf. Der Verkauf der Grundstücke ent-

forts in the Cologne bastion – their southern section today still forms the borders of the Villa Marienburg park.

In 1880, after only five years, Ernst Leybold gave up the Marienburg as his private residence. The sale of the villa lots was progressing only slowly – and evidently even he found traveling to town difficult and uncomfortable. He moved back to Cologne.

Leybold assigned title to the Marienburg development to a group of real estate companies in which he held an interest. When choosing a farm manager to run the manor estate from then on, Leybold's companies had a lucky hand. For the man in question succeeded in making the Marienburg one of the most popular travel destinations in Cologne and the environs, apart from the Botanical Gardens. The success was so enduring that a horse-and-carriage service started operating between Cologne and the Marienburg, and paddle steamers also stopped there.

It was not until the 1890s that the building development Leybold had so ardently championed started gradually to take shape. At long last the Cologne city walls were razed, and having been corseted tight for decades, the Rhenish metropolis now swiftly spread out. The new Cologne downtown arose.

The substance of the Villa Marienburg was first radically changed following a fire in 1890. The rebuilding work was undertaken in line with the plans of architect Josef Crones, with the focus now mainly on the villa's commercial use as a travel destination. Hitherto two stories high, the villa was now given a third story. Crones added wings with terraces on both sides, as well as a spacious ballroom. On the Rhine side, two turret-like corner oriels were built on the main building. The façade was then ornamented with rich Renaissance decorations. A mighty gable emphasized the building's central axis.

A round lantern adorned the stairwell in the Western wing, which also provided access to the belvedere on the roof. The latter offered a marvelous view out across the Rhine and deep into the heart of Bergisches Land opposite. The new-look villa was then given highly visible advertising in the form of a sign on the roof proclaiming »Marienburg, Hotel-Pension«. On the side facing away

wickelte sich nur schleppend. Außerdem war offenbar selbst für ihn der Weg in die Stadt zu beschwerlich und unbequem. Er zog wieder nach Köln.

Das Eigentum an den Marienburger Grundstücken übertrug Leybold auf Immobilienfirmen, die ihm anteilig gehörten. Bei der Auswahl des Ökonomen, der das Landgut von nun an betreiben sollte, bewiesen die Firmen Leybolds eine glückliche Hand. Ihm gelang es, die Marienburg zu einem der beliebtesten Ausflugsziele Kölns und der Umgebung zu machen – neben der Flora. Der Erfolg war offensichtlich so nachhaltig, daß eine Pferdebahn von Köln zur Marienburg eingerichtet wurde und auch Raddampfer die Marienburg anliefen.

Die gewünschte und erhoffte rege Bautätigkeit setzte erst in den 90er Jahren ein. Endlich fiel die Kölner Stadtmauer, und die jahrzehntelang eingeschnürte rheinische Metropole dehnte sich mit hoher Dynamik aus. Die Kölner Neustadt entstand.

Eine erste einschneidende bauliche Veränderung erfuhr die Villa Marienburg infolge eines Brandes um das Jahr 1890. Der Wiederaufbau wurde nach den Plänen des Architekten Josef Crones durchgeführt, wobei nun die kommerzielle Nutzung als Ausflugsziel im Vordergrund stand. Das bisher zweigeschossige Haus wurde um ein Stockwerk erweitert. Beidseitig fügte Crones ebenerdig ausladende Flügel mit Terrassen und einem geräumigen Festsaal an. Zum Rhein hin erhielt der Bau zwei turmartige Eckerker. Die Fassade wurde mit reichen Renaissance-Dekorationen verziert. Ein mächtiger Giebel betonte die Mittelachse des Hauses.

Eine runde Laterne schmückte das Treppenhaus der Westfassade, das auch den Zugang zum Belvedere des Daches ermöglichte. Von hier aus hatte man einen großartigen Blick auf den Rhein bis weit in das Bergische Land. Der neu gestaltete Bau wurde auf dem Dach mit der gut sichtbaren Werbung »Marienburg, Hotel-Pension« versehen. Auf der vom Rhein abgewandten Seite der Marienburg gab es einen Kinderspielplatz, Karussells, Schaukeln und zeitweise auch einen Kirmesbetrieb. In der Werbung für das »Hotel-Restaurant 1. Ranges und Pension« hieß es ca. 1892:

from the Rhine, the Marienburg boasted a children's playground, roundabouts, swings, and even, at one point, a little fair. In the ads for the »First-Class Hotel-Restaurant and Pension« produced around 1892 we read:

»From all sides it is the most beautiful and pleasant point on the Rhine below Bonn, offering the most marvelous prospects - recognized and also recommended by renowned physicians for its pure, refreshing air. Expansive, shady parks and promenades, protected verandas and terraces, elegantly furnished rooms with balconies and a glorious view of the Rhine River through as far as the Siebengebirge hills, bathrooms, reading rooms, playrooms, a ballroom, telephone, garden games, and tremendous military band music on Sundays and holidays... This establishment, quite unique in the region, is predestined for both longer quiet stays in the country yet closely linked to the city, and for day-trippers and festive occasions. Marienburg, nr. Cologne, G. Stark, Director.«

The populace of the Marienburg district grew from 33 persons in 1855 to over 650 in 1900. The construction boom which commenced before the century continued, with the interruption only of the First World War, through until the 1920s.

At long last, in 1905, transport arrived that did justice to the Marienburg district's needs: an electric tram. The main means of transport of the upper classes now terminated in the very middle of Marienburg, at the Südpark.

Leybold's immense financial and personal commitment had paid off in the long term, and with it the idea of an exclusive villa suburb. This can be seen all too well from the names of the owners of the real estate: entrepreneurs such as van der Zypen or Clouth, tobacco merchant Feinhals, the family of publishers NevenDuMont, department-store pioneers Cords and Tietz, as well as Stüssgen, town planner Josef Stübben, Chief Musical Director Abendroth, and famous architects such as Theodor Merrill, Schreiterer, Below, and Paul Pott.

In addition to granting lots only to inhabitants who were absolutely upper crust, the quality of residences in the suburb was also maintained by strict rules written into the title deeds. They included

»Allseitig als schönster, aussichtsreichster und angenehmster Punkt am Rhein, unterhalb Bonn, anerkannt und auch von ärztlichen Autoritäten wegen seiner reinen, erfrischenden Luft empfohlen. Ausgedehnte, schattenreiche Parkanlagen und Promenaden, geschützte Veranden und Terrassen, elegant ausgestattete Fremdenzimmer mit Balconen und prächtiger Aussicht auf den Rheinstrom bis zum Siebengebirge, Bade-, Lese- und Spielzimmer, Festsaal, Telephon, Gartenspiele, an Sonn- und Feiertagen vorzügliche Militär-Conzerte ... Dieses in seiner Art hier einzige Etablissement empfiehlt sich sowohl zu längerem, ruhigem Landaufenthalt in engster Verbindung mit der Grosstadt, als auch zu Ausflügen und Festlichkeiten. Köln-Marienburg. G.Stark, Director.«

Die Bevölkerung Marienburgs war von 33 Personen im Jahr 1855 bis ins Jahr 1900 auf über 650 Personen gewachsen. Der Bauboom, der noch vor der Jahrhundertwende einsetzte, dauerte – nur unterbrochen vom ersten Weltkrieg - bis ins zweite Jahrzehnt des 20. Jahrhunderts.

1905 kam endlich das Verkehrsmittel, das dem Anspruch der Marienburger Bevölkerung gerecht wurde: die elektrische Straßenbahn. Das Hauptverkehrsmittel der gehobenen Schichten hatte seine Endstation jetzt mitten in Marienburg am Südpark.

Daß sich Leybolds enormes finanzielles und persönliches Engagement lohnte und die Idee einer exklusiven Villenkolonie langfristig aufging, zeigen die Namen der Grundstückseigentümer: die Unternehmer van der Zypen und Clouth, der Tabakhändler Feinhals, die Verlegerfamilie NevenDuMont, die Kaufhauspioniere Cords und Tietz sowie Stüssgen, der Stadtplaner Josef Stübben, Generalmusikdirektor Abendroth und bekannte Architekten wie Theodor Merrill, Schreiterer, Below und Paul Pott.

Über die Prominenz der Bewohner hinaus sollte die Wohnqualität Marienburgs durch strenge Regeln grundbuchlich gesichert werden. Dazu gehörten das Verbot jeglicher Berufsausübung, natürlich ausgenommen die Tätigkeiten der Hausangestellten in den großbürgerlichen Villenhaushalten, und jegliche industrielle oder gewerbliche Grundstücksnutzung. Das Verbot ging so weit, daß

a prohibition on any profession being exercised on the premises, with the natural exception of the butlers and servants in the grand villas, as well as any industrial or commercial use of the real property. The ban was so comprehensive, that even lawyers and doctors were forbidden to open offices and merchants were prohibited from setting up shop. All supplies thus had to be brought in from Bayenthal

On February 10 1907, Ernst Leybold died. He had been able to witness at least the early successes of his life's work.

auch Rechtsanwälten und Ärzten untersagt war, ihre Praxen zu unterhalten, und Kaufleuten nicht gestattet war, Läden einzurichten. Zur eigenen Versorgung war man auf Bayenthal angewiesen und ließ sich von dort Waren liefern.

Ernst Leybold starb am 10. Februar 1907. Immerhin hatte er noch die Anfänge des Erfolges seines Lebenswerkes erlebt.

Ernst Leybold im Alter von 60 Jahren
Ernst Leybold, age 60

Villenkolonie Köln Marienburg
Villa estate in Marienburg, Cologne

Marienburg mit neuer Pferdebahn und Schiffsanlegestelle
Marienburg, with new coach station and a quay for steamers

Ansicht der erweiterten Marienburg um 1893
View of the extended district of Marienburg around 1893

»Gruß von der Marienburg«
»Greetings from the Marienburg«

Chapter 3
1906: Heinrich Schütte becomes owner

In April 1906, Heinrich Schütte, owner of the Alfred C. Schütte machine factory in the Poll district of Cologne, acquired Villa Marienburg and the grounds of the park from the Kölnische Immobiliengesellschaft for 590,000 marks. He commissioned Bonn-based architect and Royal Architectural Councilor Anton Wingen to mastermind converting the building for his private use - and expanding it quite considerably.

Wingen's plans entailed two outwardly almost identical two-story wings being added to the central building, both with attics beneath the roofs. They bring to mind the spirit of French architects and feature not only Baroque but also many »Empire« elements among the ornamentation. In the same vein, the main building was revamped, specifically the windows, additional decoration was added, and the gables and the oriel facing on to the Rhine were redesigned. The interior with its numerous salons was reminiscent of the French flair of the Empire period, with paneling made of precious woods. The heart of the house was now a large, completely white music room, flanked on two sides by smaller salons. A spacious salon with a wintergarden rounded the building off to the South. At the North end there was a dining room with oak paneling, ornamented additionally with gold-embossed leather wallpaper, and the kitchens with the servants quarters and ancillary rooms. What was striking was the combination of true-to-style French Empire ornamentation and »heavy« German interior design from the turn of the century. All the stucco work in and on the building was handled by the Cologne firm Hans Hunzinger. Of special note are the curved iron window crosses which have survived to the present, and emphatically influenced the building's style. The new construction work also included

Kapitel 3
1906: Heinrich Schütte wird Eigentümer

Im April 1906 erwarb Heinrich Schütte, Inhaber der Maschinenfabrik Alfred C. Schütte in Köln-Poll, von der Kölnischen Immobiliengesellschaft für 590.000 Mark die Villa Marienburg mit dem Parkgelände. Er ließ sie durch den Bonner Architekten und königlichen Baurat Anton Wingen für seine privaten Zwecke prunkvoll - einem Schloß ähnlich - umbauen und erheblich erweitern.

Nach seinen Plänen wurden an beiden Seiten des Kernbaus zwei äußerlich nahezu gleiche, zweigeschossige Flügel mit Mansardendächern angefügt. Sie erinnern an den Geist französischer Architektur und weisen neben barocken Elementen auch viele Empire-Dekorationen auf. In diesem Sinne wurde auch der Kernbau überarbeitet - vor allem im Bereich der Fenster – sowie der Giebel und der Erker zur Rheinseite neu gestaltet. Das Innere mit seinen zahlreichen Salons zeigte französischen Flair mit Empire-Einbauten und Vertäfelungen aus wertvollen Hölzern. Zentrum des Hauses bildete von nun an das große, ganz in weiß gehaltene Musikzimmer, das seitlich von zwei kleineren Salons flankiert wurde. Ein großzügiger Salon mit dem davorliegenden Wintergarten schloß das Gebäude nach Süden hin ab. Im Norden befanden sich der eichengetäfelte Speiseraum, der zusätzlich durch eine goldgeprägte Ledertapete geschmückt war, und die Küchenräume mit Personal- und Nebenräumen. Bemerkenswert war das Nebeneinander von stilgerechten Empire-Dekorationen und »schwerer« deutscher Inneneinrichtung der Gründerzeit. Sämtliche Stuckarbeiten im und am Haus wurden von der Kölner Firma Hans Hunzinger ausgeführt. Herausragend sind die geschwungenen Fensterkreuze aus Eisen, die bis heute erhalten sind und den Stil des Hauses maßgeblich beeinflussen.

Zu den Neubauarbeiten zählten auch die Remisengebäude an

the outhouses on the Western borders of the grounds, which included stables and living quarters for the gardens and coachmen, a larger glasshouse complex complete with a house for palms, and a new rose-garden. The grounds' fencing was also new, with a magnificent wrought-iron gate with a fountain in front of it. Ever since, the latter has formed the decorative welcoming entrance to the Marienburg when approached from Parkstrasse.

The side adjoining the banks of the Rhine was redesigned to feature a »Baroque« stairway sporting terraces and balustrades, affording a little privacy for what was now once more a personal residence.

Sadly, the family did not have the pleasure of living for long in its glorious house. Ten years after they had moved in, it was confiscated in 1918 by the English Army, which set up the HQ there for the Commanding Officer of the Occupying Forces. And with the rampant inflation of the 1920s, the Schütte era at the Marienburg came to an end.

der westlichen Grundstücksgrenze - mit Stallungen und Wohnräumen für Gärtner und Kutscher, einem größeren Gewächshauskomplex mit Palmenhaus und einem neuen Rosengarten. Neu errichtet wurde auch die Grundstückseinfriedung mit dem großartigen schmiedeeisernen Tor und davor ein Brunnen. Dieser stellt seither den dekorativen Auftakt zur Marienburg von der Parkstraße aus dar.

Der Zugang vom Rhein her wurde durch eine »barocke« Treppenanlage umgestaltet, die mit ihren Terrassen und Balustraden auch ein wenig Sichtschutz für das nun wieder private Anwesen bot.

Leider war der Familie kein langer Aufenthalt in ihrem prächtigen Haus gegönnt. Bereits 10 Jahre nach Bezug des Hauses wurde es 1918 für den Oberkommandierenden der britischen Besatzungsmacht beansprucht und beschlagnahmt. Mit der Inflation endete auch die Ära Schütte als Eigentümer.

Die Marienburg nach dem Umbau zum Privathaus für die Familie Schütte   The Marienburg after

ted into the Schütte family's private residence

Schütte vor dem Eingangsportal der Marienburg
Schütte outside the entrance to the Marienburg

Parkansicht im Winter
View of the park in winter

Aufgang zur Marienburg von der Rheinseite
Broad path up to the Marienburg from the Rhine

Tänzerinnen im Park   Dancers in the park

Das Musikzimmer   The music room

Herrensalon zwischen Speise- und Musikzimmer um 1913
Gentlemen's drawing room, between the dining and music rooms around 1913

Großer Salon, später das Kaminzimmer   Grand salon, later the living room with fireplace

Der kleine Salon neben dem Musikzimmer
The small salon next to the music room

Wintergarten mit großem bleiverglasten Fenster
Wintergarden with large leaded-glass windows

Chapter 4
1926: Robert Gerling moves into the Marienburg

On November 22 1922, Robert Gerling purchased the premises for the price of 41 million marks, a figure attributable to the breakneck inflation of the day - despite the fact that the English Army still held it confiscated and he could therefore initially not move into it. Not until the English left at the beginning of 1926 was the villa free and, only then following thorough redecoration and a certain amount of modernization could Robert and Auguste, their sons Robert, Hans, Walter, and their poodle Stropp move into the house. Robert Gerling commissioned the Cologne company of Heinrich Pallenberg to undertake the modernization. Almost all the »Empire« decorations were removed, and the interior redesigned to the company's own plans - in the style of a German Renaissance.

The music room was outfitted with richly decorated wooden paneling along the walls and ceiling, while the remaining rooms received highly patterned textile wallpaper framed by wooden paneling, not to mention armchairs and carpeting boasting the same pattern. The entire ground floor was taken up with the Gerling living rooms and also served representative purposes. The three sons had their bedrooms on the first floor of the Northern wing, whereby the eldest son was given the larger, middle room, and his brothers Hans and Walter had their rooms either side. The room positioned centrally opposite the stairway and featuring the large terrace towards the Rhine was used by the family as their breakfast room and also as a private living room. The parent's dressing room and bedroom was in the first floor of the Southern wing. The top floor was given over to a salon, guestrooms, the sons' studies, and servant quarters.

The large park was landscaped after the English model and was now outfitted with a large swimming pool - it was shaped to resem-

Kapitel 4
1926: Robert Gerling bezieht die Marienburg

Robert Gerling erwarb am 22.11.1922 das Anwesen für den In-
flationspreis von 41 Millionen Mark, obwohl er den von der
englischen Besatzungsmacht noch immer beschlagnahmten Bau
zunächst selbst nicht nutzen durfte. Erst mit dem Abzug der Engländer zu Beginn des Jahres 1926 wurde die Villa frei und konnte nach
gründlicher Sanierung und einigen Umbauten von Robert und Auguste Gerling, den Söhnen Robert, Hans, Walter und dem Pudel
»Stropp« bezogen werden. Mit den Umbauten beauftragte Robert
Gerling die Kölner Firma Heinrich Pallenberg. Sie entfernte fast alle
Empire-Dekorationen und ersetzte sie durch Innenausbauten nach
eigenen Plänen im Stile einer deutschen Renaissance.

Das Musikzimmer wurde mit einer reich verzierten Holztäfe-
lung an Wänden und Decke versehen, die übrigen Räume erhielten
stark gemusterte, durch Holzpaneele gefaßte Textiltapeten und
ebenso stark gemusterte Sessel und Teppichböden. Das gesamte Erdgeschoß enthielt die Wohnräume der Familie und diente der Erfül-
lung von Repräsentationspflichten. Die drei Söhne hatten ihre
Schlafzimmer im Nordflügel im ersten Stock, der älteste das größte
mittlere Zimmer — flankiert von seinen Brüdern Hans und Walter.
Der zentral gegenüber der Treppe liegende Raum mit der großen
Terrasse zum Rhein wurde von der Familie als Frühstücks- und
wohl auch als privater Wohnraum genutzt. Die Eltern hatten ihre
Ankleide- und Schlafzimmer im südlichen Flügel des ersten Stocks.
Das Dachgeschoß beherbergte einen Salon, die Gästezimmer, die
Arbeitszimmer der Söhne und einige Personalzimmer.

Im weitläufigen Park, nach englischem Muster angelegt, wurde
ein großes Schwimmbecken gebaut, dessen Form an einen natürli-
chen Teich erinnert. Die drei Söhne nutzten den Park zum Spielen.

ble a natural pond. The three sons used the park as their playground. They could even row a boat on the pool, and there was an artificial brook with a lock, and down on the river bank a boathouse complete with motor boats.

The mood of life at the Marienburg is best reflected in an entry dating from December 1929 which Hans Gerling made in his diary: »In the afternoon prior to Christmas Eve we walked in great expectation up and down the corridor in front of the room containing the presents. Everywhere, lamps were radiant, decked out in Christmas glory. In the quiet of other rooms we recited the poems once again, and Aunt Ida, Mother's sister, listened to make sure we had learned them well. We had Christmas carols played, Robert playing piano, and then the present-giving started. We took the white linen cloths down from the doors of the reception room in which the Christmas tree stood. The day before we had ourselves decorated it, and now the electric candles were gleaming brightly. We sang three carols ... Aunt Ida played the piano. Then the maids were led to their tables. Soon they had gazed at everything in wonder and carried their gifts away. Then the family was alone.«

Robert Gerling died in 1935. His widow at first continued to reside in the large house with her three sons, but soon the boys were to go their own ways.

Auf dem Schwimmbad wurde Boot gefahren, es gab einen künstlichen Bach mit Schleuse und unten am Rhein ein Bootshaus mit Motorbooten.

Leben und Atmosphäre auf der Marienburg spiegelt ein Eintrag in Hans Gerlings Tagebuch vom Dezember 1929 wider: »Am Nachmittag vor Heiligabend gingen wir unruhig im Flur vor dem Bescherungszimmer auf und ab. Überall strahlten weihnachtlich geschmückte Lampen. Im Stillen sagten wir nochmals die Gedichte auf, und Tante Ida, Mutters Schwester, mußte uns abhören. Wir ließen Weihnachtslieder spielen, Robert spielte Klavier, und dann begann die Bescherung. Wir nahmen die weißen Leinentücher von den Türen des Empfangszimmers, in dem der Weihnachtsbaum stand. Tags vorher hatten wir ihn eigenhändig geschmückt, und jetzt strahlten die elektrischen Kerzen in vollem Glanz. Wir sangen drei Weihnachtslieder ... Tante Ida spielte Klavier. Dann wurden die Dienstmädchen zu ihren Tischen geführt. Bald hatten sie alles bewundert und weggetragen. Darauf waren wir für uns.«

Robert Gerling verstarb im Jahre 1935. Seine Witwe lebte zunächst weiter in dem großen Haus mit ihren drei Söhnen, die jedoch bald eigene Wege gehen sollten.

Robert Gerling 1930

Die drei Söhne von Robert Gerling 1926
Robert Gerling's three sons in 1926

»Bootsfahrt« im Schwimmbad (von links: Robert, Pudel »Stropp«, Hans und Walter)
»Boat trip« on the swimming pool (l. to r.: Robert, »Stropp« the poodle, Hans, and Walter)

Vor dem Sprung (von links: Robert, Hans und Walter)
Ready to jump (l. to r.: Robert, Hans, and Walter)

Hans Gerling, 1935

Robert Gerling mit Tanten
Robert Gerling with his aunts

Eingang
Entrance

Pavillon
pavilion

Pudel »Stropp«
»Stropp« the poodle

Das Leben auf der Marienburg fotografiert von Hans Gerling

Treibhausanlage
Glasshouses

Platanengruppe
Group of plane trees

Hausansicht
view of the house

Robert Gerling mit Frau Auguste
Robert Gerling and his wife Auguste

Das Musikzimmer zur Zeit von Robert Gerling
The music room at the time of Robert Gerling

Das Musikzimmer mit Dekokamin
The music room with decorative fireplace

Chapter 5
1942: Hans and Irene Gerling –
A residence and a place of work

Robert Gerling junior emigrated to the United States in 1938. After the outbreak of the Second World War, Hans Gerling was stationed in Hamburg and then in Copenhagen as a soldier. His younger brother Walter took part in the Russian campaign. Thus, Auguste Gerling lived on her own in the Marienburg. Irene Uhrmacher and Hans Gerling married in September 1942, although he had to remain in active service in the army until 1945. Before the war was over, their first daughter Helen had been born, and from then on Irene and Helen lived in the Marienburg and, on occasion in a small unobtrusive country house in Oeldorf, which seemed safer.

During one of the numerous English bombing raids, which primarily targeted the nearby Rodenkirchen Bridge, the Marienburg also took a hit. The firebomb went straight through the roof and various ceilings, landing finally in the grand piano which stood in the second-story living room. The piano immediately went up in flames and it was not possible to extinguish it so that the fire was able to spread swiftly. In desperation, Irene Gerling ran down to the Rheinuferstrasse to get help. She courageously took up a stance in the middle of the road and flagged down a fire engine which was en route to another fire. With the words: »The Marienburg is on fire! If you come and put it out you can have the contents of the wine cellar,« she saved her house from catastrophe. The firemen immediately took up the offer, first putting paid to the fire, and then to the wine cellar. The Marienburg was saved.

Despite further attacks and taking a few more hits, the manor emerged from the massive bombing of Cologne relatively unscathed. Only the third story had been completely destroyed. The

Kapitel 5
1942: Hans und Irene Gerling –
Ein Haus zum Wohnen und Arbeiten

Robert Gerling junior war 1938 in die USA ausgewandert. Nach Ausbruch des Zweiten Weltkrieges war Hans Gerling in Hamburg und Kopenhagen als Soldat stationiert. Sein jüngerer Bruder Walter nahm indessen am Rußlandfeldzug teil. So lebte Frau Auguste Gerling allein in der Marienburg. Irene Uhrmacher und Hans Gerling heirateten im September 1942, obwohl dieser bis 1945 bei der Wehrmacht dienen mußte. Noch in der Kriegszeit wurde ihre erste Tochter Helen geboren. Deshalb bewohnten Mutter und Tochter die Marienburg und zeitweise ein kleines und unauffälliges Landhaus in Oeldorf, das ihnen sicherer erschien.

Bei einem der zahlreichen Bombenangriffe der Engländer, die in erster Linie der nahegelegenen Rodenkirchener Brücke galten, wurde auch die Marienburg getroffen. Die Brandbombe durchschlug mit großer Kraft Dach und Fußböden und landete im Flügel, der im Wohnraum der zweiten Etage stand. Dieser fing sofort Feuer und war nicht mehr löschbar, so daß sich der Brand schnell ausbreiten konnte. In der Not lief Irene Gerling hinunter zur Rheinuferstrasse, um Hilfe zu holen. Mutig stellte sie sich mitten auf die Straße und hielt winkend einen Feuerwehrzug an, der auf dem Weg zu einem Einsatz war. Mit den Worten: »Die Marienburg brennt! Wenn Ihr löschen kommt, könnt Ihr den Weinkeller haben« bewahrte sie ihr Haus vor einer Katastrophe. Die Feuerwehrmänner nahmen ihr Angebot an. Sie löschten zuerst das Haus und dann den Weinkeller. Die Marienburg war gerettet.

Trotz weiterer Angriffe und Treffer hat das Anwesen die massiven Bombardements von Köln relativ unversehrt überstanden. Lediglich das dritte Obergeschoß wurde komplett zerstört. Die Stadt

city, by contrast, had been razed to the ground. Germany was beaten. And Marienburg was ready to see occupying forces again.

»The Villa Marienburg likewise looks despondent; the park has been ploughed by at least nine direct hits; the house itself also took two or three hits, not to mention the grenades from artillery fire. Nevertheless, the villa was immediately occupied by US troops and was no-go for any of us for five weeks. The furniture, to the extent that it still existed and had not been crushed, was then transported off, probably to outfit the planned officers' quarters.« This was how Hans Gerling remembered those times.

Hans and Irene Gerling started immediately after the War to have the roof and interior restored and to furnish it in keeping with their own tastes. With the Gerling Group's commercial success they increasingly used the house for representative purposes. In 1952, the ground floor was renovated. The large living room was awarded a marble fireplace and a mahagony trimming for the silk wallpaper. An apartment for their grandmother was established on the second story, who lived there until her death in 1964. In 1954, the bedroom was renovated and a new children's room created. In 1956, an elevator was built between the ground and attic floors and, in 1960, the large indoor swimming pool in the garden story.

In 1968, together with architect Hanns Koerfer some thought was put into the idea of restoring the uppermost floor and the gables on the Rhine side which had been destroyed in the bombing raids. To this end, alternative plans were also devised, and tested on full-size scale models. However, Hans Gerling did not like any of them, perhaps owing to their design or perhaps simply because he shied away from the noise and dirt of building work. He therefore opted for a less extensive solution. In 1968, in the space of only six weeks, a complete new roof was put up. Taking its cue from the old Marienburg, the new roof involved slate-clad pointed turrets over the two protruding oriels on the corners of the building front facing the Rhine; they were tipped with fluting ornamented zinc sheet. The roof was given a new balustrade edge made of closed ornamented sections and a row of bal-

lag jedoch in Schutt und Asche. Deutschland war besiegt. Die Marienburg sah ihre zweite Besatzungsmacht.

»Die Villa Marienburg sieht ebenfalls trostlos aus; der Park ist wie umgepflügt durch mindestens neun Volltreffer; das Haus selbst hat auch zwei oder drei Bomben bekommen, abgesehen von den Granaten beim Artillerie-Beschuß. Trotzdem wurde die Villa sofort von amerikanischen Truppen belegt und war fünf Wochen lang für jeden gesperrt. Die Möbel, soweit sie noch vorhanden und nicht zertrümmert waren, sind dann abgefahren worden, vermutlich zur Einrichtung der vorgesehenen Offizierswohnungen.« So die Erinnerung von Hans Gerling.

Hans und Irene Gerling begannen unmittelbar nach dem Krieg, das Dach und den Innenausbau des Hauses wieder instand zu setzen und gemäß ihren Vorstellungen auszubauen. Sie nutzten mit dem geschäftlichen Erfolg des Konzerns das Haus wieder vermehrt zu Repräsentationszwecken. 1952 wurde das Erdgeschoß renoviert. Das große Wohnzimmer erhielt einen Marmorkamin und eine Mahagonieinfassung für die Seidentapeten. Eine Wohnung für die Großmutter wurde im zweiten Obergeschoß ausgebaut, in der sie bis zu ihrem Tode im Jahr 1964 lebte. 1954 wurden die Schlafzimmer renoviert und ein neues Kinderzimmer geschaffen. 1956 baute man einen Aufzug zwischen Erd- und Dachgeschoß und 1960 das große Innenschwimmbad im Hanggeschoß.

1968 wurde gemeinsam mit dem Architekten Hanns Koerfer überlegt, das im Krieg verlorene Dachgeschoß mit rheinseitigem Giebel wieder aufzubauen. Zu diesem Zweck wurden alternative Pläne erarbeitet und mit Modellen im Maßstab 1:1 getestet. Keiner der Entwürfe gefiel jedoch dem Hausherrn, vielleicht aus Gründen der Gestaltung, vielleicht aber auch, weil er Lärm und Schmutz der Bauarbeiten scheute. Und so entschied er sich für eine kleine Lösung: 1968 wurde in nur 6 Wochen ein komplett neuer Dachausstieg erstellt. Nach dem Vorbild des alten Hauses Marienburg wurden über den beiden seitlichen Erkervorsprüngen an der Rheinfassade verschieferte Turmspitzen errichtet, die als Krönung getriebene und verzierte Zinkblechspitzen erhielten. Der Dachrand bekam eine

usters. The occasion was also used to eliminate other war damage on the façade toward the Rhine.

For Hans Gerling, this was the house in which he had grown up - it was both the heart of the family, and also a place where he worked, thought, and received Gerling employees. He set up his office and the room where he received staffers in the wintergarden - which had been expanded in the summer of 1969 to include a glazed pavilion and served Hans Gerling as a room with a view, a room for contemplation, and a room to meet staff members. What was back then an ultra-modern glass-and-steel structure led direct to the family living room on the first floor.

The ground floor primarily served representative functions. *Salons*, corridors, and halls were all designed in the 1960s style and outfitted with a comprehensive collection of modern art. Bright yellow and a strong red predominated - on the walls, the furniture, and the lampshades. The family regularly used the high table in the dining room, likewise on the ground floor, when Hans Gerling was present. Otherwise Irene Gerling and her children took their meals at a round table in the room's oriel.

The parent's rooms were located in the southern wing on the upper story, while the rooms in the northern wing belonged to the children, Helen, Brita, Dany, and Rolf. On the West side, a small tea kitchen was installed - evidently the entire family's favorite room, where they were able to cook for themselves and enjoy a relaxed evening.

Hans and Irene Gerling's family continued life in the tradition of Robert Gerling and celebrated Christmas Eve along with their domestic staff. The Christmas tree was in the music room, the gifts for the domestic staff placed each in its traditional position. Hans Gerling read from the Christmas tale, Irene Gerling played carols on the grand piano, and everyone sang. Then the staff collected their presents and the family continued their celebrations alone.

Irene Gerling died in 1990, and Hans Gerling followed her a year later. An important chapter in the history of the Marienburg thus came to a close.

neue Balustrade aus geschlossenen Schmuckelementen und Balusterreihen. Bei dieser Gelegenheit wurden auch weitere Kriegsschäden an der Rheinfassade beseitigt.

Für Hans Gerling war dieses Haus, in dem er aufgewachsen war, sowohl Zentrum der Familie, als auch ein Ort, an dem er arbeitete, nachdachte und Mitarbeiter empfing. Er richtete sein Arbeits- und Empfangszimmer im Wintergarten ein, der im Sommer 1969 um einen gläsernen Pavillon erweitert wurde und dem Hausherrn gleichermaßen als Aussichts-, Kontemplations- und Empfangsraum diente. Von dort führte damals eine hochmoderne Glas-/Edelstahlkonstruktion direkt in das Familienwohnzimmer im 1. Stock.

Das Erdgeschoß diente vorwiegend der Repräsentation. Salons, Flure und Hallen wurden im Stil der 60er Jahre gestaltet und enthielten eine umfangreiche Sammlung moderner Kunst. Es dominierten helles Gelb und kräftiges Rot - sowohl an Wänden, als auch auf Möbeln und Lampenschirmen. Im Speisezimmer, ebenfalls im Erdgeschoß, benutzte die Familie den großen Tisch im Speisezimmer, wenn Hans Gerling anwesend war. Ansonsten speisten Mutter und Kinder an einem runden Tisch im Erker des Zimmers.

Im Obergeschoß lagen im Süd-Flügel die Zimmer der Eltern, daran anschließend im Nord-Flügel die Räumlichkeiten der Kinder Helen, Brita, Dany und Rolf. An der Westseite wurde eine kleine Teeküche eingebaut - dem Vernehmen nach der Lieblingsraum der ganzen Familie, wo man selbst kochen und einen zwanglosen Abend verbringen konnte.

Die Familie Hans und Irene Gerling setzte die Tradition von Robert Gerling fort und feierte den heiligen Abend zusammen mit den Hausangestellten. Der Weihnachtsbaum stand im Musikzimmer, die Geschenke für das Personal waren für jeden an seinem angestammten Platz aufgebaut. Hans Gerling las aus der Weihnachtsgeschichte vor, Irene Gerling spielte am Flügel Weihnachtslieder, und alle sangen dazu. Danach holten sich die Angestellten ihre Geschenke, und die Familie feierte alleine weiter.

Irene Gerling verstarb im Jahre 1990 und ein Jahr später Hans Gerling. Eine bedeutende Ära des Hauses Marienburg ging zu Ende.

Ein Spaziergang im Park mit den Dalmatinern »Honey« und »Percy«
Walking in the park with »Honey« and »Percy«, both Dalmatians

Die Marienburg nach einem Bombenangriff im Zweiten Weltkrieg: Das Hauptdach und
Dachgeschoß sind bis auf den Giebel zerstört
The Marienburg after a World War II bombing raid – with the exception of the gables,
the main roof and attic have been destroyed

Blick durch den Giebel
View through the gables

Die »fensterlose« Südfassade
The »blind« south facade

Brunnen vor dem Eingangstor, Parkstraße 55
Fountain in front of the entrance gate on Parkstraße 55

Westfassade der Marienburg nach dem Zweiten Weltkrieg
West facade of the Marienburg after World War II

Remise mit Garage und Personalwohungen 1960
Coach house, including the garage and staff accommodation 1960

Parkansicht mit Schwimmbad um 1960
View of the park and swimming pool around 1960

Das Hallenbad
The indoor pool

Irene und Hans Gerling in der Teeküche
Irene and Hans Gerling in the small private kitchen

Kleiner festlicher Tisch im Speisezimmer
Small table laid for a festive occasion in the dining room

Schreibtisch von Hans Gerling im alten Wintergarten
Hans Gerling's desk in the old wintergarden

Das Kaminzimmer, früher der große Salon
The living room with fireplace, previously the grand salon

Das Musikzimmer um 1975
The music room around 1975

Blick aus dem erweiterten Wintergarten 1970
View from the wintergarden after the extension work, 1970

Chapter 6
1992: The Gerling Group Corporate Home

R olf Gerling placed the Marienburg at the disposal of the Gerling Group in 1992 – as a training center for upper-level exec-
utives and for representative functions. The »Marienburg Seminars«
saw the light of day - soon to become a fixed and important compo-
nent in the Gerling Group's management training program.

The wide-ranging management training program addresses a va-
riety of themes, ranging from important aspects of the insurance industry through to corporate culture and the paradigm shift in modern society.

To this end, the Marienburg was completely renovated. The representative rooms on the ground floor more or less retained their
function and furniture. They now house a private collection of out-
standing examples of 20th century art, as well as rooms for meetings,
chats, and celebrations.

Ever since 1908, no changes have been made to the impressive
dining room. With its dark oak paneling beneath the embossed and
gold-plated leather wallpaper, and an oak ceiling with five heavy
chandeliers, it conveys a true impression of the original magnificent
turn-of-the-century dining room. The upper stories have been divid-
ed into three seminar areas, each with two group rooms and one
main room. All of the rooms are designed to use ultra-modern seminar and conference technology. The swimming pool annex on the
garden floor is now a multi-purpose room and is used for larger lec-
tures and press conferences. The outhouses were converted into a
new guest house strictly in line with the preservation under which
they stand. It has 25 guest rooms, all of which have been furnished
with the greatest attention to use of the healthiest materials possible.
The entire building now boasts oiled oak parquet, the beds do not

Kapitel 6
1992: Das »Corporate Home« des Gerling-Konzerns

Rolf Gerling stellte 1992 die Marienburg dem Konzern als Bildungszentrum für obere Führungskräfte und für Repräsentationsaufgaben zur Verfügung. Die »Marienburger Seminare«, ein fester und wichtiger Bestandteil des Bildungsprogramms für das Management des Gerling-Konzerns, wurden aus der Taufe gehoben.

Das breit angelegte Management-Bildungsprogramm behandelt eine Vielzahl von Themen. Diese reichen von wichtigen Aspekten der Versicherungsbranche bis hin zur Unternehmenskultur und zum Paradigmawechsel.

Zu diesem Zweck wurde die Marienburg vollständig renoviert. Die repräsentativen Räume im Erdgeschoß behielten weitgehend ihre Funktion und auch ihr Mobiliar. Sie beherbergen nun eine private Sammlung von herausragenden Beispielen der Kunst des 20. Jahrhunderts sowie Räume zum Treffen, Plaudern und Feiern.

Der eindrucksvolle Speiseraum ist seit 1908 unverändert. Er vermittelt mit einer dunklen Eichenvertäfelung unterhalb einer geprägten und vergoldeten Ledertapete, einer Eichendecke mit fünf schweren Kristalleuchtern den originalen Eindruck eines prachtvollen Speiseraums der Gründerzeit. Die Obergeschosse wurden in drei Seminarbereiche mit je zwei Gruppen- und einem Hauptraum eingeteilt. Alle Räume lassen modernste Seminar- und Tagungstechnik zu. Der Schwimmbadanbau im Hanggeschoß ist heute ein Mehrzweckraum und wird für größere Vortragsveranstaltungen und Pressekonferenzen verwendet.

Der Umbau der Remise zum neuen Gästehaus fand unter strengen Auflagen des Denkmalschutzes statt. Seine 25 Gästezimmer wurden zudem unter Verwendung möglichst gesunder Materialien ausgestattet. Das gesamte Haus ist durchgängig mit einem geölten

have any metal parts, and the wooden surfaces have been given a protective coat of wax. Unlike those in the Marienburg, the rooms are decidedly plain and straightforward. There was a deliberate choice not to hang art on the walls. Nothing is allowed to interfere with the ascetic mood of tranquility the rooms exude.

The history of the Marienburg is truly one of fascinating change - from manor house, travel destination, family residence, to that of training center, guesthouse and corporate home of the Gerling Group. Many are the people who have filled the house with life. Many are the destinies that have led people here.

★

We can only hope that the entrepreneurial spirit which has resided at the Marienburg from the outset will continue to engage the minds of the staff and visitors to this hospitable house - to the benefit of everyone.

Sources
Wolfram Hagspiel, »Köln: Marienburg,« vol. 2, ed. City of Cologne, (Cologne, 1996).
Minna Leybold, »Geschichte der Familie Leybold,« (Rothenburg on the Tauber, 1931).
Sigrid Müller, »Villa war auch Ausflugslokal,« in: »Kölner Stadtanzeiger,« Feb. 27, 1986.
Wolf v. Niebelschütz: »Robert Gerling - Ein dramatisches Kapitel deutscher Versicherungsgeschichte,« (Tübingen, 1954).
Joachim Römer, »Leybolds Notizen zur Stadtgeschichte. Die Marienburg,« ed. by Ernst Leybold Immobilien, (Cologne, undated).

Eichenparkett ausgelegt, die Betten sind ohne Verwendung von Metallteilen gebaut, die Holzoberflächen werden durch eine Wachsschicht vor Beschädigung geschützt. Die Zimmer sind im Gegensatz zu den Räumen der Marienburg einfach und schlicht. Auf die Ausstattung mit Kunst wurde hier bewußt verzichtet. Die Ruhe und die Kargheit der Schlafräume soll durch nichts gestört werden.

Die Geschichte der Marienburg war und ist bewegt - vom Landgut, Ausflugsort und Familiensitz bis zum Bildungszentrum, Gästehaus und Corporate Home des Gerling-Konzerns. Viele Menschen und Schicksale haben das Haus mit Leben erfüllt.

★

Es bleibt zu wünschen, daß der unternehmerische Geist, der in der Marienburg von Anbeginn wohnte, auch in Zukunft auf die Mitarbeiter und Besucher des gastlichen Hauses zum Wohle des Ganzen ausstrahlt.

Quellen

Wolfram Hagspiel: Köln: Marienburg, Bd. II (hrsg. v. Stadt Köln), Köln 1996.

Minna Leybold: »Geschichte der Familie Leybold«, Rothenburg o. T. 1931.

Sigrid Müller: »Villa war auch Ausflugslokal«, in: Kölner Stadtanzeiger vom 27.2.1986.

Wolf v. Niebelschütz: Robert Gerling – Ein dramatisches Kapitel deutscher Versicherungsgeschichte. Tübingen 1954.

Joachim Römer: Leybolds Notizen zur Stadtgeschichte, Die Marienburg (hrsg. v. Ernst Leybold Immobilien), Köln o. J.

Rolf Gerling: Die Marienburg als Bildungszentrum und Corporate Home des Gerling-Konzerns
Rolf Gerling: the Marienburg as a training center and as Gerling Group's corporate home

Seminarraum im ersten Obergeschoß
First-floor seminar room

Seminarraum im zweiten Obergeschoß
Second-floor seminar room

Das Musikzimmer im Jahr 2000
The music room, 2000

Kaminzimmer mit Bildern von Karl Hofer
Living room and fireplace, with pictures by Karl Hofer

Die Marienburg im Schatten der mächtigen Platanen
The Marienburg, in the shade of giant plane trees

Die deutsche Bibliothek – CIP Einheitsaufnahme
Die Marienburg : Leben und Geist eines Hauses = The Marienburg / hrsg. von Rolf Gerling. –
München : Gerling-Akad.-Verl., 2001
ISBN 3-932425-37-5

Copyright © 2001, Gerling Akademie Verlag GmbH,
Prinzregentenstraße 11, D-80538 München.
Alle Rechte, insbesondere das Recht der Vervielfältigung
und Verbreitung, vorbehalten
Gestaltung: Claus Seitz, München
Abbildungen, soweit nicht anders verzeichnet, Gerling-Konzern-Archiv, Köln
Satz und Lithos: Fotosatz Reinhard Amann, Aichstetten
Druck und Bindung: Friedrich Pustet GmbH, Regensburg
ISBN 3-932425-37-5
www.gerling-academy-press.com